WHY WE NEED LAWS

Bertram Wilberforce

New York

Published in 2009 by The Rosen Publishing Group, Inc.
29 East 21st Street, New York, NY 10010

Book Design: Daniel Hosek

Photo Credits: Cover © GeoM/Shutterstock; cover (background) © VanHart/Shutterstock; folio background
(gavel) © Rob Marmion/Shutterstock; p. 5 © Monkey Business Images/Shutterstock; p. 7 © Time Life
Pictures/Getty Images; pp. 8–9 © Edward Gooch/Hulton Archive/Getty Images; pp. 10–11, 13 © MPI/Hulton
Archive/Getty Images; p. 15 © Jonathan Larsen/Shutterstock; p. 17 © AFP/Getty Images; p. 19 © Getty
Images; p. 20 © Sonya Etchison/Shutterstock; p. 21 © Andrew Yahin/Shutterstock.

Library of Congress Cataloging-in-Publication Data

Wilberforce, Bertram.
  Why we need laws / Bertram Wilberforce.
      p. cm. — (Real life readers)
  Includes index.
  ISBN: 978-1-4358-0135-6
  6-pack ISBN: 978-1-4358-0136-3
  ISBN 978-1-4358-2977-0 (library binding)
  1. Law—United States—Juvenile literature. I. Title.
  KF387.W525 2009
  349.73-dc22
                                    2008036742

Manufactured in the United States of America
CPSIA Compliance Information: Batch #WR016180RC: For Further Information contact Rosen Publishing, New York, New York at 1-800-237-9932

Contents

A World Without Laws

Can you imagine a world without laws? No one would use money. People could take other people's things. We could be robbed of our food, clothes, and favorite games. People could drive cars as fas as they wanted without stopping at lights and signs. People could hurt each other. We would have no government.

Without laws, people could do what they wanted. Life would be confusing and full of danger. There would be no **punishments**.

Laws exist to **protect** us from the dangerous actions of other people. Laws also help people get along together. In this book, we'll take a look at different kinds of laws, how they're made, and the effects they have on us.

People young and old need to obey laws. Laws make ▶ sure that you attend school until you are a certain age.

Laws of the Past

Laws have been around for almost as long as people have lived together. Some laws from ancient Egypt are over 5,000 years old!

King Hammurabi (ham-uh-RAHB-ee) of **Babylonia** made some of the most famous ancient laws. He ruled Babylonia from about 1790 B.C. to 1750 B.C. During that time, he had 282 laws written in stone and displayed for all to see. These laws were called the Code of Hammurabi. His people believed their gods gave Hammurabi the laws to govern. Without laws, Hammurabi couldn't have ruled his kingdom. The laws were a way to join together the people from the different lands he ruled.

However, the punishments for breaking Hammurabi's laws weren't always fair. Some people were punished more than others for breaking the same law. Wealthy people were often treated more kindly than poor people. Punishments ranged from paying money to death.

This picture shows Hammurabi (standing) receiving his laws from the god Shamash. According to one law, a man who knocked out another man's teeth would have his own teeth knocked out as punishment! ▶

Laws played an important part in American history. Under King George III, some British laws required American colonists to pay taxes on goods such as tea. A tax is money collected by the government. The colonists became angry that they had to pay taxes without having anyone to **represent** them in the British government.

Do you know what the colonists did? On December 16, 1773, colonists in Boston dressed themselves as Native Americans. They

boarded British ships that had arrived with tea and dumped the tea into Boston Harbor. This event, called the Boston Tea Party, told the British that the colonists thought the tax was unfair. Later, the colonists fought a war against the British. They won their freedom and formed a new country—the United States.

This picture is an artist's idea of the Boston Tea Party. The event shows that people often fight laws they believe are unfair. ▼

The U.S. Constitution

Each country has its own set of laws. Some countries put their most important laws into a written **constitution**. The highest law in the United States is the U.S. Constitution. That means all laws in the United States must follow the laws in the Constitution.

The Constitution was written in 1787 when the United States was a young country. Its writers wanted to join the states under one large government. Some believed that if the states had laws that were

This painting shows the early leaders of the U.S. government meeting to sign the Constitution. ▼

very different from each other, they couldn't act as one country. The government created by the Constitution has three branches. One branch is headed by the president, one by Congress, and one by the **Supreme Court**. All the parts work together, and none is more powerful than the other.

Each state in the United States has its own constitution, too. State constitutions have laws that are special to that state but still agree with the U.S. Constitution.

In 1791, Congress added the **Bill of Rights** to the Constitution. These are ten rights that belong to all citizens of the United States. The Bill of Rights was created so the government wouldn't have too much power over the people. No law can be made to take away these rights.

One right states that people don't have to let soldiers stay in their homes, as British soldiers had stayed in colonists' homes. The right to free speech means that people can say what they want—even bad things about the government—without punishment. Some countries don't have these rights. In those countries, the government can take people's homes and punish the people for what they say.

Over the years, the Constitution has been changed. Some rights were added or changed. All changes to the Constitution are called **amendments**. One amendment gave slaves their freedom; another gave women the right to vote.

This is a copy of the Bill of Rights written in 1789. It shows twelve rights. However, only ten rights were approved in 1791. ▶

12

Congrefs OF THE United States

begun and held at the City of New-York, on

Wednesday the fourth of March, one thousand seven hundred and eighty nine.

THE *Conventions of a number of the States, having at the time of their adopting the Constitution, expressed a desire, in order to prevent misconstruction or abuse of its powers, that further declaratory and restrictive clauses should be added: And as extending the ground of public confidence in the Government, will best ensure the beneficent ends of its institution.*

RESOLVED *by the Senate and House of Representatives of the United States of America, in Congress assembled, two thirds of both Houses concurring, that the following Articles be proposed to the Legislatures of the several States, as amendments to the Constitution of the United States, all, or any of which Articles, when ratified by three fourths of the said Legislatures, to be valid to all intents and purposes, as part of the said Constitution; viz.*

ARTICLES *in addition to, and amendment of the Constitution of the United States of America, proposed by Congress, and ratified by the Legislatures of the several States, pursuant to the fifth Article of the original Constitution.*

Article the first... *After the first enumeration required by the first Article of the Constitution, there shall be one Representative for every thirty thousand, until the number shall amount to one hundred, after which the proportion shall be so regulated by Congress, that there shall be not less than one hundred Representatives, nor less than one Representative for every forty thousand persons, until the number of Representatives shall amount to two hundred, after which the proportion shall be so regulated by Congress, that there shall not be less than two hundred Representatives, nor more than one Representative for every fifty thousand persons.*

Article the second... *No law, varying the compensation for the services of the Senators and Representatives, shall take effect, until an election of Representatives shall have intervened.*

Article the third... *Congress shall make no law respecting an establishment of religion, or prohibiting the free exercise thereof; or abridging the freedom of speech, or of the press; or the right of the people peaceably to assemble, and to petition the Government for a redress of grievances.*

Article the fourth... *A well regulated militia, being necessary to the security of a free State, the right of the people to keep and bear arms, shall not be infringed.*

Article the fifth... *No soldier shall, in time of peace be quartered in any house, without the consent of the owner, nor in time of war, but in a manner to be prescribed by law.*

Article the sixth... *The right of the people to be secure in their persons, houses, papers, and effects, against unreasonable searches and seizures, shall not be violated, and no Warrants shall issue, but upon probable cause, supported by oath or affirmation, and particularly describing the place to be searched, and the persons or things to be seized.*

Article the seventh... *No person shall be held to answer for a capital, or otherwise infamous crime, unless on a presentment or indictment of a Grand Jury, except in cases arising in the land or naval forces, or in the Militia, when in actual service in time of War or public danger; nor shall any person be subject for the same offence to be twice put in jeopardy of life or limb; nor shall be compelled in any criminal case to be a witness against himself, nor be deprived of life, liberty, or property, without due process of law; nor shall private property be taken for public use, without just compensation.*

Article the eighth... *In all criminal prosecutions, the accused shall enjoy the right to a speedy and public trial, by an impartial jury of the State and district wherein the crime shall have been committed, which district shall have been previously ascertained by law, and to be informed of the nature and cause of the accusation; to be confronted with the witnesses against him; to have compulsory process for obtaining witnesses in his favor, and to have the assistance of counsel for his defence.*

Article the ninth... *In suits at common law, where the value in controversy shall exceed twenty dollars, the right of trial by jury shall be preserved, and no fact tried by a jury, shall be otherwise re-examined in any court of the United States, than according to the rules of the common law.*

Article the tenth... *Excessive bail shall not be required, nor excessive fines imposed, nor cruel and unusual punishments inflicted.*

Article the eleventh... *The enumeration in the Constitution, of certain rights, shall not be construed to deny or disparage others retained by the people.*

Article the twelfth... *The powers not delegated to the United States by the Constitution, nor prohibited by it to the States, are reserved to the States respectively, or to the people.*

ATTEST,

Frederick Augustus Muhlenberg, *Speaker of the House of Representatives.*

John Adams, *Vice President of the United States, and President of the Senate.*

John Beckley, *Clerk of the House of Representatives.*

Sam. A. Otis, *Secretary of the Senate.*

How National Laws Are Made

A law begins with an idea. The idea is told to a government leader in one of the two houses, or parts, of Congress—the Senate or House of Representatives. The Senator or House member writes down the idea and why it should be a law. The idea is now called a bill.

Next, the bill is read to the Senate or House, depending on where the Congress member serves. It's then printed up for other Congress members to read. After a number of days, the bill is sent to a special **committee**. For example, a bill about pollution might go to a committee that studies pollution's effect on our health.

The committee decides if the bill should be changed in any way. It then votes on whether the bill should go on to the next step. If the committee agrees with the bill, it goes back to the Senate or House. It may be changed again.

Congress is divided into the Senate and the House of Representatives. Each state has two senators. The number of representatives a state has depends on its population. Both houses meet in the Capitol building, shown here.

After the members of the Senate or House talk about the bill and make changes to it, they vote on it. If more than half the members vote for the bill to become a law, it's sent to the other house of Congress. It may be changed again before it's voted on. The House and Senate must agree on the words in the bill before it can move to the next step.

If more than half of both the House and the Senate vote for the bill, it goes to the president. The president can sign the bill into law. He can also **veto** the bill. If the president vetoes the bill, it goes back to Congress. Congress can change the bill and send it back to the president, or they can let it die. They can also make it law without the president's agreement if two-thirds of both houses of Congress vote to do that.

16

Two-thirds of the Senate is 67 members and two-thirds ▶ of the House is 290 members. Without that many votes, the bill can't become a law after a veto.

HOW A BILL BECOMES A NATIONAL LAW

A member of Congress creates a bill and reads it to the House or Senate.

The bill goes to a committee where it's carefully looked over. It may be changed.

The committee votes whether the bill should be sent to the whole House or Senate. If the committee passes the bill, it goes back to the House or Senate.

The bill may be changed again before the House or Senate votes on the bill.

If the House or Senate passes the bill, it's sent to the other house of Congress. It may be changed again.

The other house votes for the bill. If it passes, it goes to the president.

The president may sign the bill into law or veto it. If the president vetoes the bill, it can still be passed if two-thirds of Congress vote for it.

17

All Kinds of Laws

Now you know how laws are made that everyone in the United States must follow. Your state and local laws are made in a certain way too. There are laws for every area of life. Some deal with the people's role in the government. For example, voting laws protect people's right to choose their Congress, president, and other leaders. Voters should carefully choose the leaders who create and vote for laws.

Criminal laws deal with subjects like harming or robbing someone. Why do you think these laws are so important? They keep us safe from people who wish to hurt us. Other kinds of laws deal with protecting people's property or promises people make. Still others protect people's inventions and ideas.

What kinds of laws have you heard of? Are there any laws you'd like to change?

People charged with not following a law have ▶ a right to defend themselves in court. Some courtrooms look like the one shown here.

19

The Law and You

It's important to study laws that are different in different places. For example, in the United States and Canada, people drive on the right side of the road. In some countries, people drive on the left side. You need to know these laws before driving in those countries!

Remember that you make a difference in what laws are made. Laws come from ideas. Anyone, young or old, can have a good idea. Anyone can write to their government

▲

Laws requiring people to use seat belts in cars protect us in case of accidents.

eader and suggest a law. If you want a law made so that people won't itter in your neighborhood park, just ask! Maybe someday you'll ecome a government leader making laws to help people.

From King Hammurabi to U.S. Congress, laws are made to protect people and keep order in society. Let's look at a law, why it was made, and its effect on people, including you!

A LAW AND ITS EFFECTS

LAW
Children in the United States must attend school until a certain age. (The age is different in each state.)

↓

WHY IT'S A LAW
Children must go to school so they can learn basic skills and knowledge to prepare them for life when they get older.

↓

EFFECTS
Children learn how to read and write, and learn other skills needed in everyday life.

Glossary

amendment (uh-MEHND-muhnt) An addition or change to the U.S. Constitution.

Babylonia (baa-buh-LOH-nee-uh) An ancient kingdom once located in the country that is now Iraq.

Bill of Rights (BIHL UV RYTS) The first ten amendments to the U.S. Constitution.

committee (kuh-MIH-tee) A group of people that considers and votes on a matter.

constitution (kahn-stuh-TOO-shun) The basic laws by which a country or state is governed.

protect (pruh-TEHKT) To keep from harm.

punishment (PUH-nish-muhnt) The act of causing someone pain or loss for a crime he or she has committed.

represent (reh-prih-ZEHNT) To act for someone else.

Supreme Court (suh-PREEM KORT) The highest court in the United States.

veto (VEE-toh) To refuse to sign a bill from Congress.

Index

Due to the changing nature of Internet links, The Rosen Publishing Group, Inc., has developed an online list of Web sites related to the subject of this book. This site is updated regularly. Please use this link to access the list: http://www.rcbmlinks.com/rlr/laws